# Heirloom Quilts To Treasure

Compiled and edited by the Editors
of The Progressive Farmer Magazine

# Preface

A revival of interest in the traditional art of quilt-making caused us to collect these patterns and make them available to you.

No doubt your own ancestors used some of these designs to make quilts for warmth and also for decorative spreads. With so many lightweight, warm blankets available today we no longer need quilts for warmth but they're becoming increasingly popular as spreads, especially on antique beds or. on reproductions. Some of these quilt designs may also be made into pillow tops, chair bottoms, and other decorative items. After piecing a few blocks you will have an added respect for the nimbleness of the fingers that did so many tasks that kept the home comfortable, cheerful, and attractive.

ISBN: 0-8487-0186-0

Library of Congress Catalog Card Number: 78-150090

Manufactured in the United States of America

Fourth Printing 1982

**Heirloom Quilts To Treasure**

Cover Photograph: Pat Peacock

# Contents

# A Short History of American Quilts

Colonial winters were cold, and the log houses of the colonists drafty. But the busy English and Dutch housewife kept her scraps, pieced them together, and the members of her household did not suffer. Large, warm quilts covered the beds, heavy quilted curtains were drawn over the windows, and quilted petticoats were part of every woman's wardrobe. The English petticoat was worn in modest concealment, but the Dutch one was worn highly colored and much in sight.

The patchwork quilts were the ones of which the quiltmaker was proudest, while the piecework bed coverings were most frequent. This is not so difficult to understand when you remember that the materials had to be laboriously woven in the home, or imported. The appliqué (or patched) quilt, calling for a large unpieced background, and large pieces, was a luxury and a showpiece. But the pieced quilts, using every available scrap of new material, were constantly being made and were on every bed. The Crazy Quilt is the oldest and one of the most common of colonial pioneer days because it made use of even the tiniest and most irregularly shaped scraps.

When the quilt was "ready for the frame" it was the custom to ask the women of the neighborhood to come and help with the quilting. Thus the quiltmaking was not only a household art, born of family needs, but an interest drawing the busy women into social groups.

The patterns used, many of which have come down to us, were often inspirations of the home—Cake Stand, Windmill, Dresden Plate, and the Tea Leaf. The Bible, so large a factor in the daily life, was responsible for such names as Rob Peter To Pay Paul and Jacob's Ladder. The New World worked itself into the quilts in Bear's Paw, Crossed Canoes, Turkey Track, Log Cabin, and Arrowhead. These, and thousands of others have spread with the population and are to be found in every part of the country.

While only a very few of the many truly beautiful old quilts have been preserved, quiltmaking itself has passed from mother to daughter, and today many Southern homes and community groups are producing worthy decendants of this splendid art.

## Making a Quilt

The first thing to decide as you plan your quilt is the size. Many old quilts were three or more yards square, generous proportions being most necessary in the days when broad four posters were heaped with feather beds. But modern double beds have been standardized by the furniture companies and are 54 x 74 inches. Twin beds are 39 x 74 inches. Today then, a 90- x 108-inch quilt will be long enough to serve as an ornamental covering for the bedding, and also cover the pillows bolster fashion. A large spread for a single bed is 72 x 108 inches. If the quilt is for warmth only and is to cover but two sides and one end of the bed, it may be 72 x 90 inches for a double bed and 60 x 90 inches for a single. The best plan is to measure your bed, making allowance for the height of the mattress, and vary the size accordingly.

The border and number of blocks suggested in the pattern may be changed to meet your own requirements. A high old-fashioned four poster, for example, is quite charming with a valance, or ruffle, which in the old days was used to conceal the trundle bed.

In planning the border, keep in mind that its width must make a suitable "frame" for the design, as well as fill out the size to the proportions of the bed.

If the material is washable, you will find it worthwhile to wash and iron your material before cutting—in this way avoiding uneven shrinkage and puckers in the finished quilt.

For lasting satisfaction in your handiwork, choose materials of good quality and fast-color. Use the same quality for blocks, lining, framing, and binding, to insure long life and even wear for the finished product.

Before cutting the pieces, be sure that the pattern is true and accurate. It will be best to cut a sandpaper pattern from the paper one.

Turn the material on the wrong side and mark the exact size of the piece with a pencil or piece of chalk. Then cut a quarter inch (or whatever seam allowance you wish) outside the line, and when you come to piecing you have a guideline. Cut all pieces at the same time, and pin the groups together. Then you can remove one piece at a time as you need it.

When possible, arrange the pieces on the material so that when the patches are seamed together a bias edge will sew to a straight one. The large triangular pieces used in sewing blocks together on the bias should have the straight of the goods on the longest side.

Pieced blocks should be pressed out with the seams flat or to one side as they are finished and checked for accuracy with the pattern. Where several joints and corners come together, be very careful to make a perfect center of joining. Avoid drawn or puckered seams. Use No. 50 or 60 Cord thread.

When the top is pieced together, square the quilting frame and place the lining in first, then the cotton batting, and lastly the pieced top. Have the edges perfectly square and even, and baste on the outer edge. Then you're ready to quilt.

Quilting was invented to hold the padding in place, and elaborate patterns came as an afterthought. The simplest form is a diagonal, spaced to suit the design, and lightly drawn on the quilt with a pencil, or piece of chalk, and a ruler. The diagonal lines will show the pattern nicely, and the material is better reinforced than if the quilting were to run parallel with the weave. This diagonal may be enhanced by double and triple diagonals, diamonds, etc. Cups, saucers, and plates are also the source of many quilting patterns.

For most designs we suggest that you follow the outlines of the design. Then when the quilt is used on the lining side it will duplicate the pattern.

If the quilt is an intricate geometric design, simple straight line quilting is practically demanded. On the other hand, if the quilt consists of plain blocks used to join pieced ones, the plain blocks may have more intricate designs.

The padding comes in sheets of cotton manufactured especially for quilts, and should be of such quality that it will not pull apart when the quilt is washed. Sometimes the sheet of cotton is treated with a slightly glazed surface, so that it unrolls and unfolds like flannel and has no sticking surfaces.

Special needles, short and slender (but with large eyes), are manufactured for quilting, and the most popular sizes run from 5 to 9.

A variety of quilting transfers are sold by firms which handle needlework patterns and designs.

The quilting, done with No. 40 or 50 thread, should be started at one end, and finished at the other, with the fullness kept ahead of the work. Some of the best quiltmakers suggest the use of waxed thread for quilting.

A true bias binding, not more than one-half inch wide when finished, should be used for the edge of the quilt. If the corners of the quilt are slightly rounded a more perfect binding is possible.

When the quilt is finished, embroider your signature and the date in one corner, identifying for all time the thing of beauty on which you have spent so many pleasurable hours.

## Color Beauty for Quilts

You have probably noticed that a great many heirloom quilts make use exclusively of "oil" red, yellow, and sometimes indigo blue. These colors were believed by our grandmothers to be the only reliable and fadefast ones in cotton. However, when today's market offers such a profusion of lovely colors and shades in fast-colored fabrics, the quiltmaker may have whatever combination of colors she believes most suited to her design and most in harmony with the furnishings of the room where her quilt is to be used.

When the quilt is to be made from scraps, the quiltmaker, of course, has to do the best she can with what she has. But the amount of time and labor spent on a quilt should dictate against combining fabrics that are essentially unsuited to one another. Old-Fashioned Flower Garden and Log Cabin are good patterns to use with a miscellaneous assortment of material.

When purchasing material, it is safest to choose colors that have the same degree of intensity. For example, light green and pale yellow will go together better than dark green and pale yellow, or bright yellow and light green. But you may secure an effect of great interest and refinement by the use of subdued colors with jewel-like accents of brilliant contrast.

When a stronger color is used to give emphasis to the pattern, let it be in small quantity and carefully selected.

Several shades of the same color, if well chosen, are very pleasing.

Do not use print materials that are too large in design, as large designs cut into small pieces and combined with a solid color will give a spotty effect.

One color should be used in larger quantities than the others. This dominating color will prevent a spotty or mottled effect. Lining the quilt with one of the colors is a good way to emphasize the harmony.

Yellow, in a room, gives a sense of cheer, lightness, and space.

Blue gives a sense of calm and restfulness.

Green gives the feeling of freshness and coolness.

Red, rose, and orange give warmth, homeyness, and cheer, and should be used in rooms where there is a northern exposure.

When the room for which your quilt is planned has a sunny southern exposure, use green for a cool and restful atmosphere.

Lavender and orchid are too dead to use in large quantities, unless the room is very large and sunshiny.

# Roses of Picardy

Use your prettiest prints to make
the "roses" of this block. If you
strip the blocks together, match
your stripping with the center of
the "roses" if possible  You'll need 35 blocks.

Do Not Allow for Seams

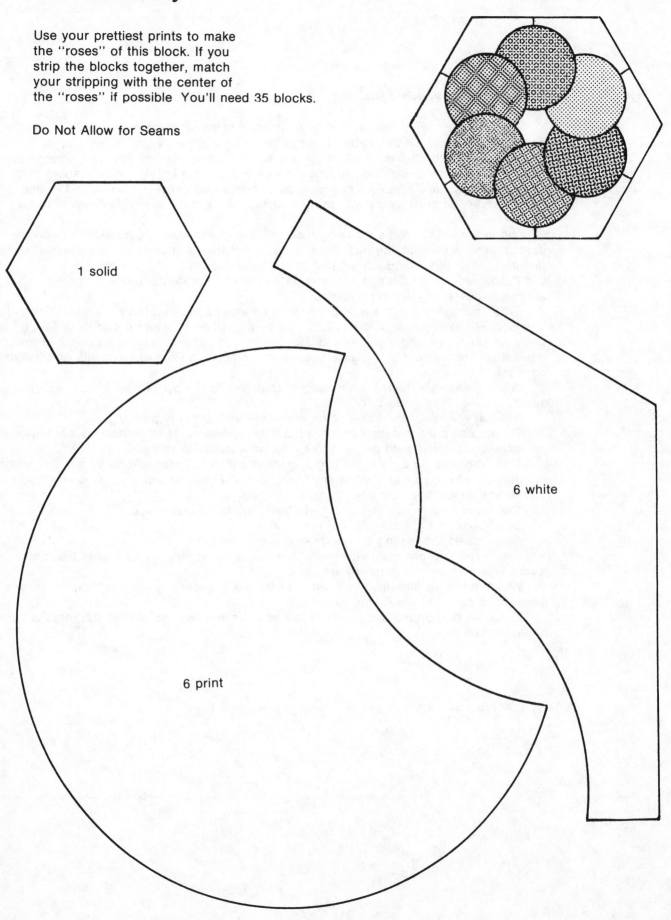

1 solid

6 white

6 print

## Our Village Green

63 squares will be required to make a quilt 90 x 108 inches, using a 3-inch border of triangles at the sides. In putting together (7 across—9 down) alternate a block with 4 light triangles at the top with one with 4 darks.

ALLOW FOR SEAMS

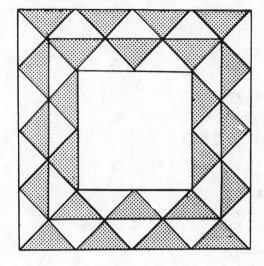

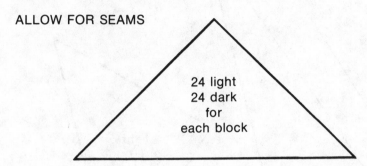

24 light
24 dark
for
each block

1 for each block

# Crossed Canoes

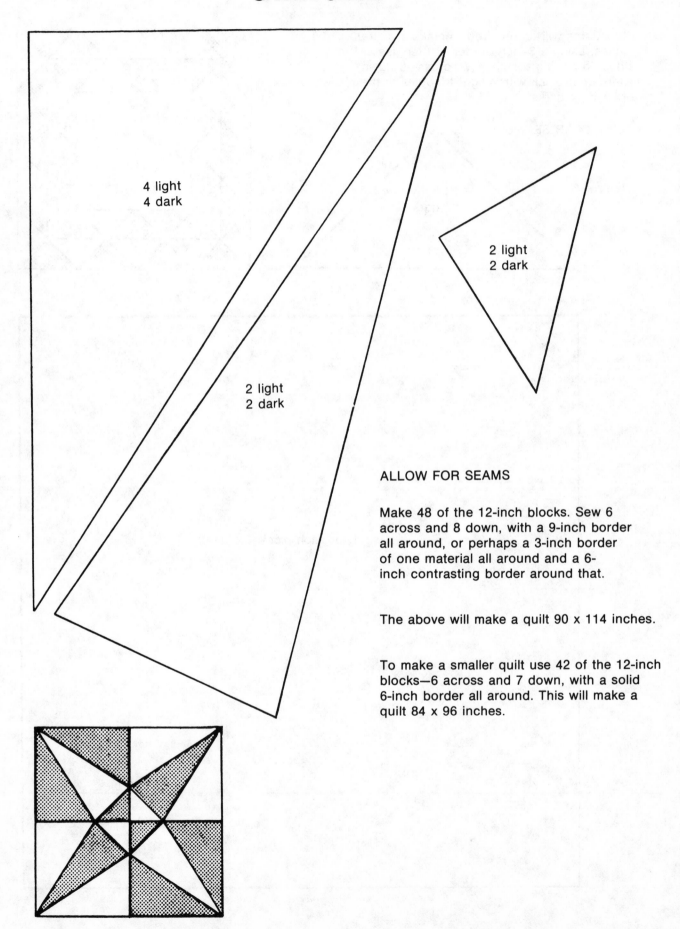

4 light
4 dark

2 light
2 dark

2 light
2 dark

ALLOW FOR SEAMS

Make 48 of the 12-inch blocks. Sew 6
across and 8 down, with a 9-inch border
all around, or perhaps a 3-inch border
of one material all around and a 6-
inch contrasting border around that.

The above will make a quilt 90 x 114 inches.

To make a smaller quilt use 42 of the 12-inch
blocks—6 across and 7 down, with a solid
6-inch border all around. This will make a
quilt 84 x 96 inches.

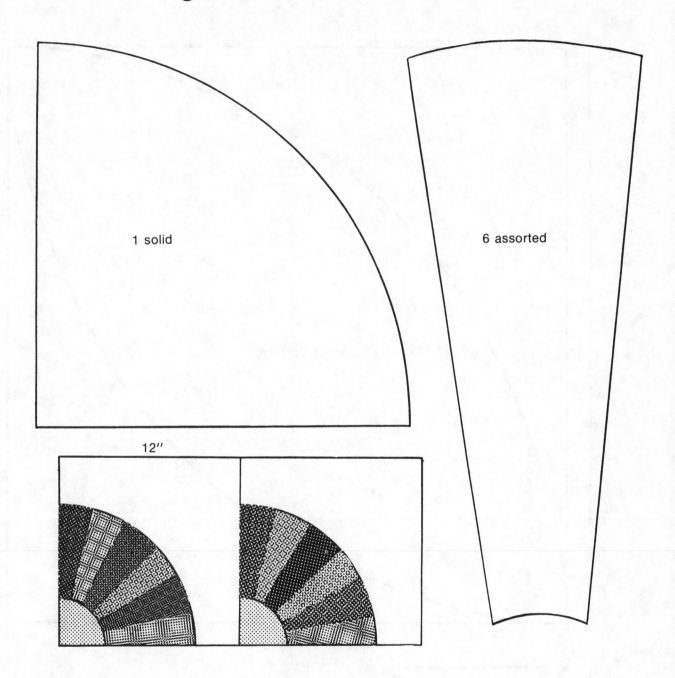

1 solid

6 assorted

12″

**ALLOW FOR SEAMS**

Make 48 of the 12-inch blocks. Sew 6 across and 8 down, with a 9-inch border all around, or perhaps a 3-inch border of one material around and a 6-inch contrasting border around that. This will make a quilt 90 x 114 inches.

To make a smaller quilt use 42 of the 12-inch blocks—6 across and 7 down, with a solid 6-inch border all around. This will make a quilt 84 x 96 inches.

Extra strips or lattice work may be used nicely with this design.

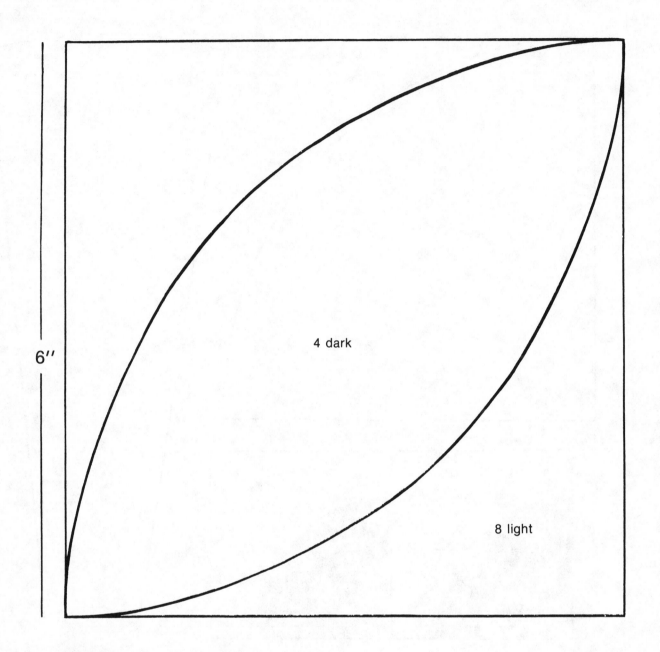

6″

4 dark

8 light

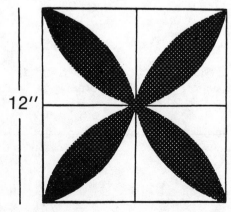

12″

Make 48 of the 12-inch squares. Sew 6 across and 8 down, with a 9-inch border all around, or a 3-inch border of one material all around and a 6-inch contrasting border around that. This will make a quilt 90 x 114 inches.

A smaller quilt may be made with 42 blocks, 6 across and 7 down, using a solid 6-inch border. When finished it will be 84 x 96 inches.

ALLOW FOR SEAMS

# Log Cabin

Make 120 blocks 8-inch square. Sew the blocks together 10 across and 12 in length. Add a 6-inch border at top and bottom and a 5-inch border at the sides, and the finished quilt will be 90 x 108 inches. To make the blocks, cut as directed and follow diagram of the square to put together.

In Canada, this is called the "ribbon block," the pieces being cut from ribbons.

ALLOW FOR SEAMS

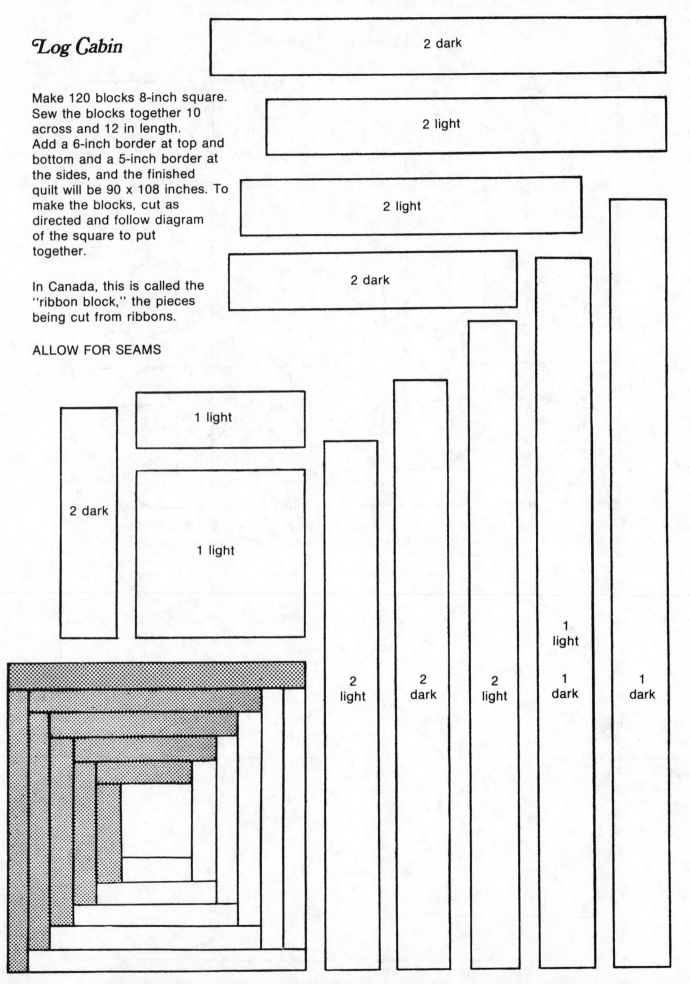

# Monkey Wrench

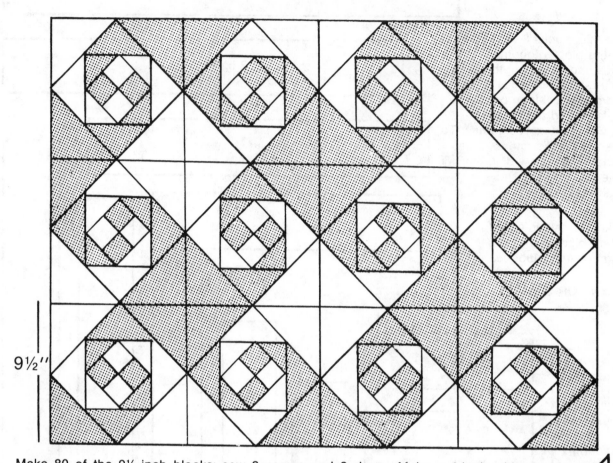

9½″

Make 80 of the 9½-inch blocks; sew 8 across and 9 down. Make a 4-inch white border all around, then a 3-inch dark border around the white. This will make a quilt 90 x 108 inches.

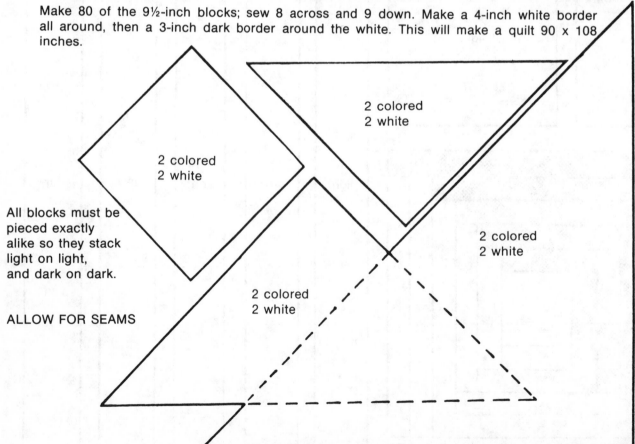

2 colored
2 white

2 colored
2 white

2 colored
2 white

2 colored
2 white

All blocks must be pieced exactly alike so they stack light on light, and dark on dark.

ALLOW FOR SEAMS

# Old-Fashioned Flower Garden

Piece the flowers first, then set together. To square up the sides of the quilt, extend some of the white hexagons as shown in the picture.

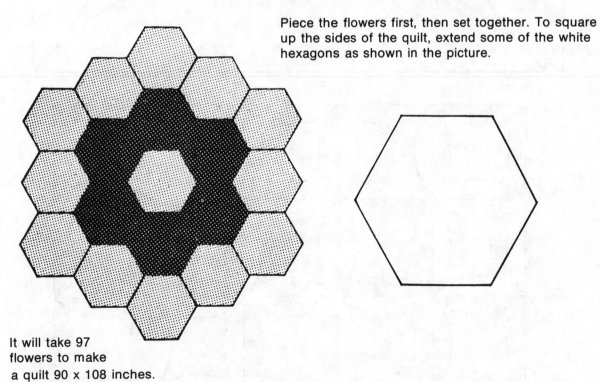

It will take 97 flowers to make a quilt 90 x 108 inches.

**ALLOW FOR SEAMS**

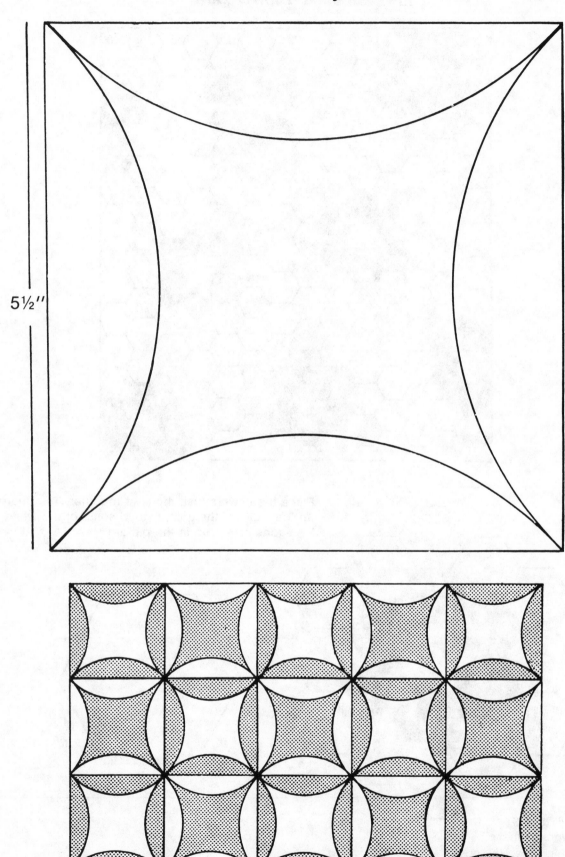

5½″

Make 238 of the 5½-inch squares. Sew together 14 across and 17 down. Then put a 7-inch border all around, making the quilt, when finished, 91 x 107½ inches.

**ALLOW FOR SEAMS**

B

A

C

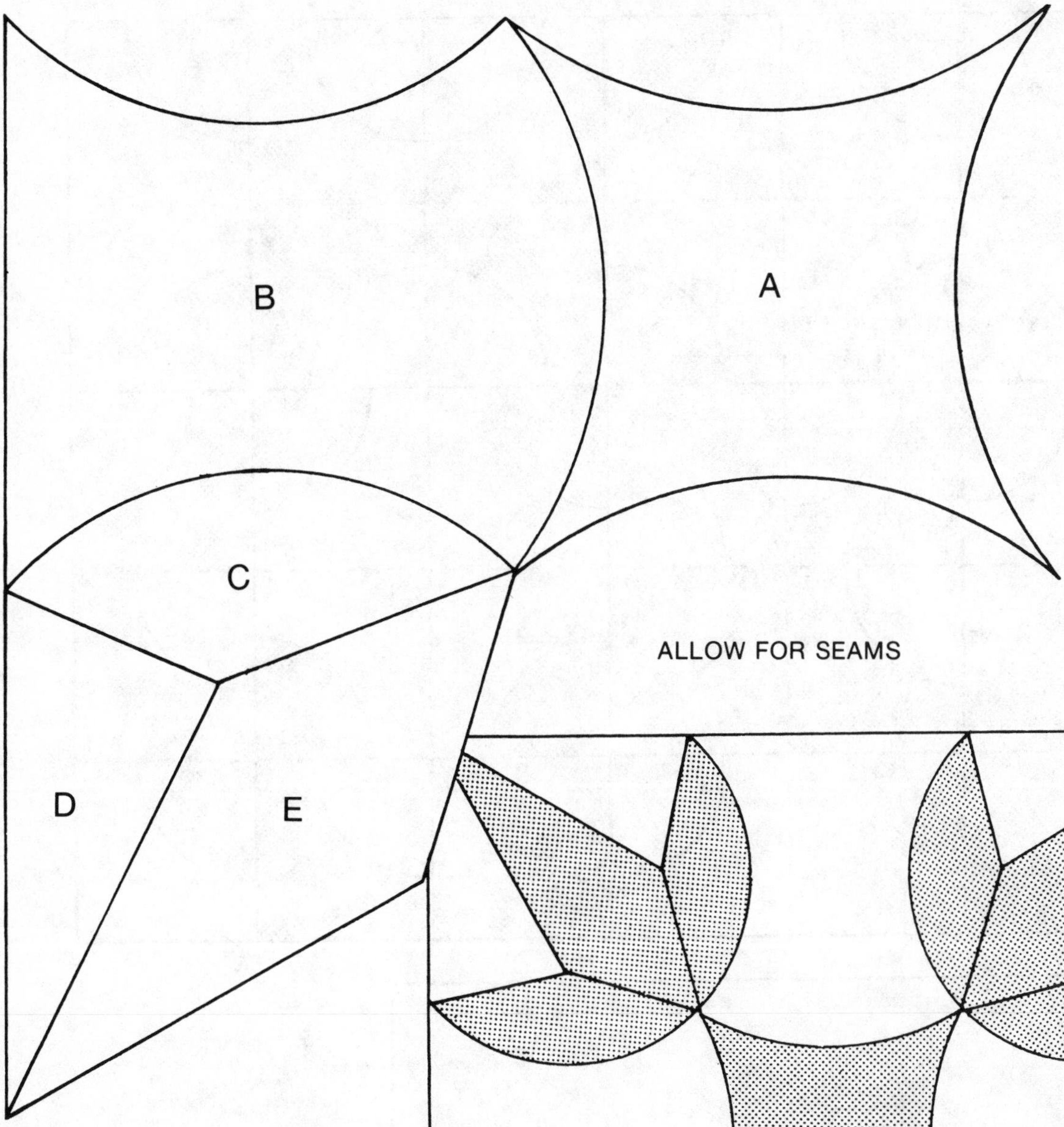

ALLOW FOR SEAMS

D

E

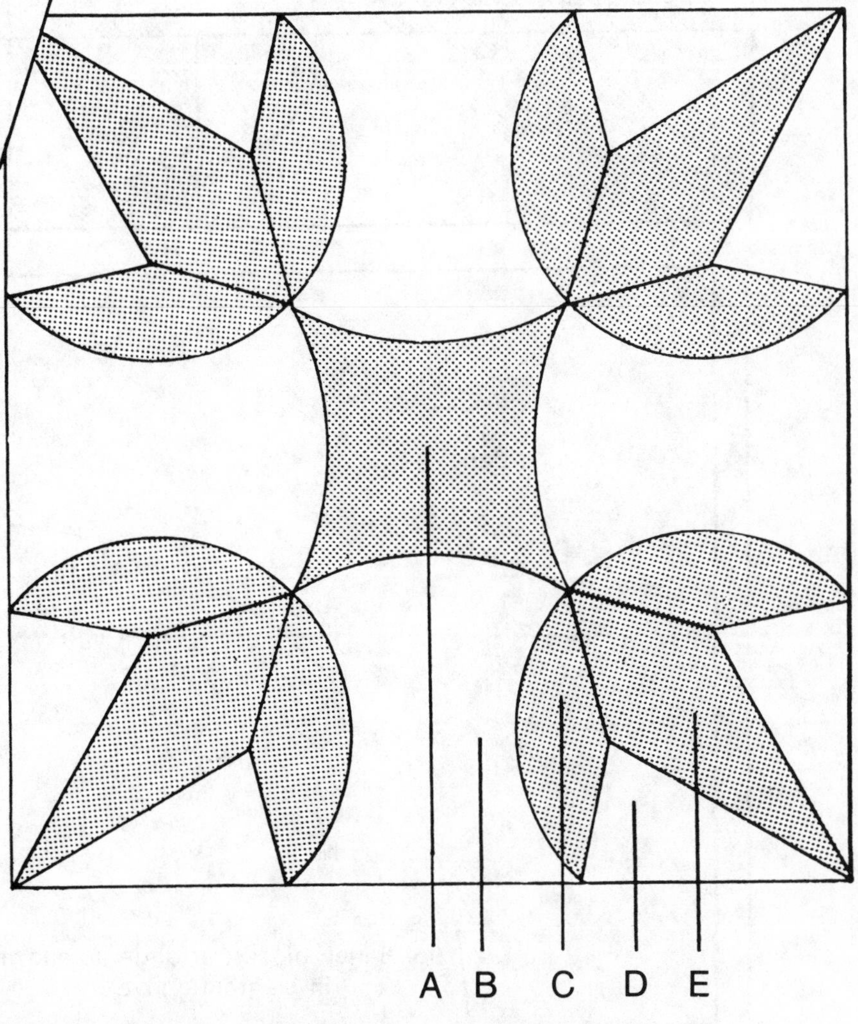

The traditional arrangement of
this design is an alternation of
plain and pieced blocks.

Make 80 blocks 9-inch square; sew
8 across and 10 down. A 9-inch
border all around will make the
finished quilt 90 x 108 inches.

A  B  C  D  E

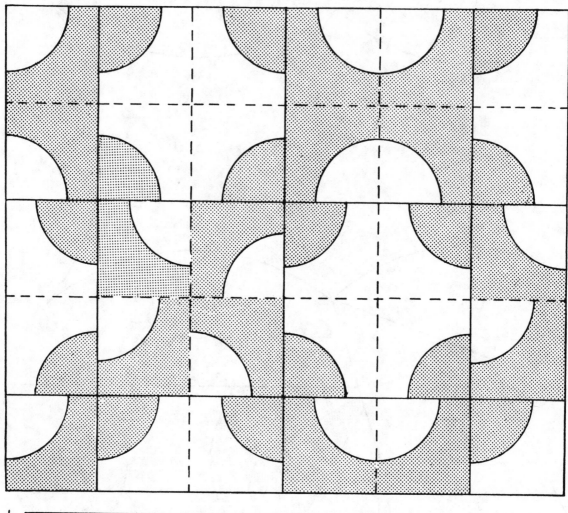

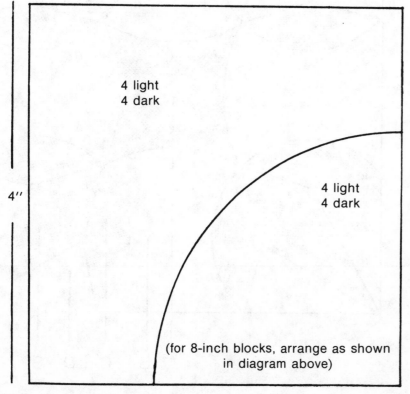

4″

4 light
4 dark

4 light
4 dark

(for 8-inch blocks, arrange as shown
in diagram above)

Make 480 of the 4-inch squares.
If 20 of these are used
across and 24 are used in
length, with a 5-inch border
all around, the finished
quilt will be 90 x 108 inches.

Many variations of this
arrangement are possible.

ALLOW FOR SEAMS

# Diamond Star

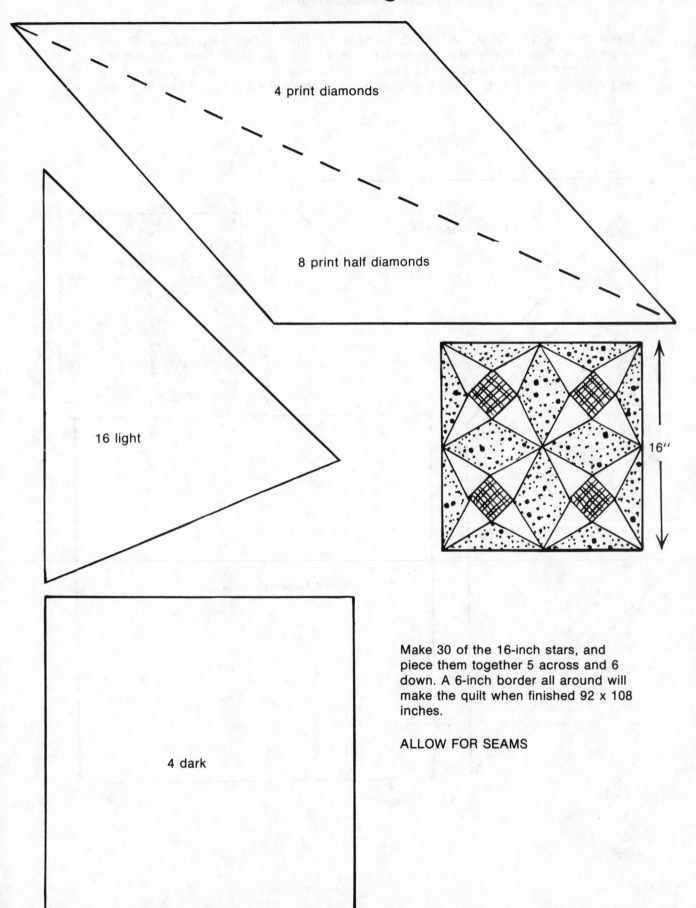

4 print diamonds

8 print half diamonds

16 light

16"

4 dark

Make 30 of the 16-inch stars, and piece them together 5 across and 6 down. A 6-inch border all around will make the quilt when finished 92 x 108 inches.

**ALLOW FOR SEAMS**

# Eight Pointed Star

Make 48 of the 12-inch blocks. Sew 6 across and 8 down, with a 9-inch border all around, or perhaps a 3-inch border of one material all around and a 6-inch contrasting border around that. Finished quilt will be 90 x 114 inches. To make a smaller quilt use 42 blocks—6 across and 7 down—with a solid 6-inch border all around. This will make a quilt 84 x 96 inches.

ALLOW FOR SEAMS

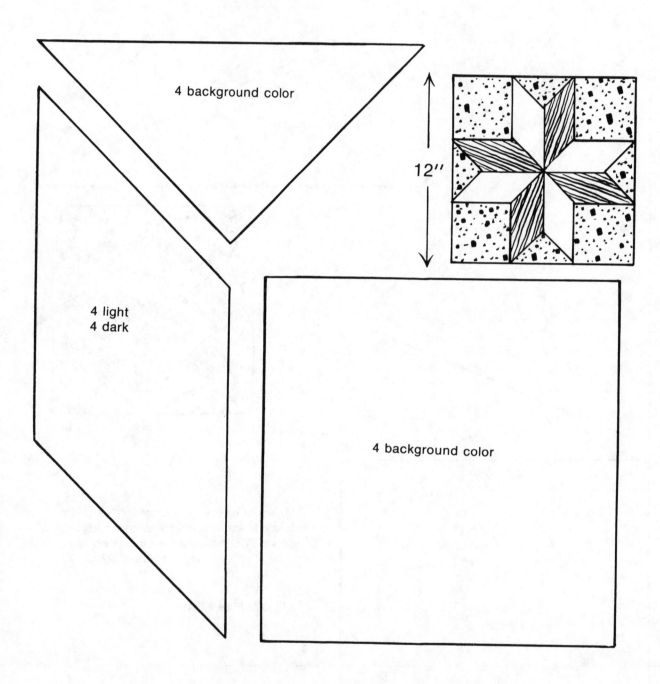

4 background color

4 light
4 dark

12"

4 background color

20

# Lone Star

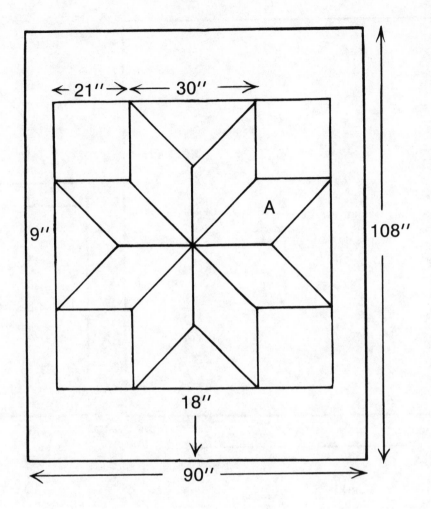

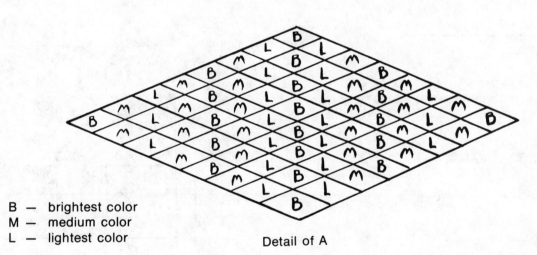

B — brightest color
M — medium color
L — lightest color

Detail of A

1 background color

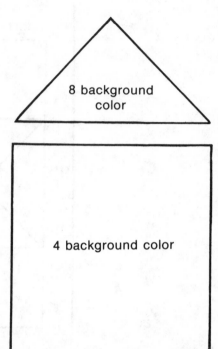

8 background color

4 background color

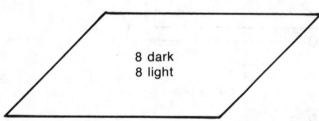

8 dark
8 light

Make 120 of the 9-inch blocks. Sew 10
across and 12 down. This, without a border,
will make a quilt 90 x 108 inches.

ALLOW FOR SEAMS

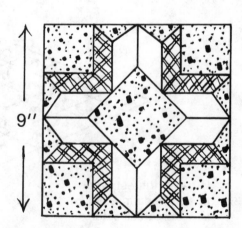

9"

# Star and Cone

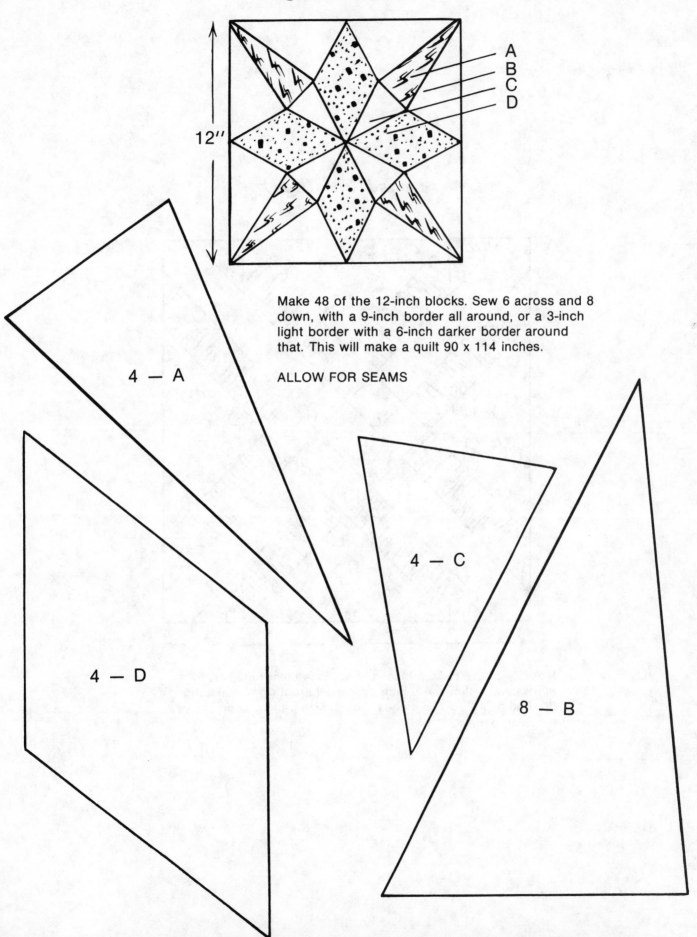

12″

A
B
C
D

Make 48 of the 12-inch blocks. Sew 6 across and 8 down, with a 9-inch border all around, or a 3-inch light border with a 6-inch darker border around that. This will make a quilt 90 x 114 inches.

ALLOW FOR SEAMS

4 — A

4 — D

4 — C

8 — B

# Star and Cross (No. 1)

← 16″ →

Make 30 of the 16-inch blocks, and piece them together, 5 across and 6 down. A 6-inch border all around will make the finished quilt 92 x 108 inches. Actual size pattern is on the following page.

# Star and Cross (No. 1)

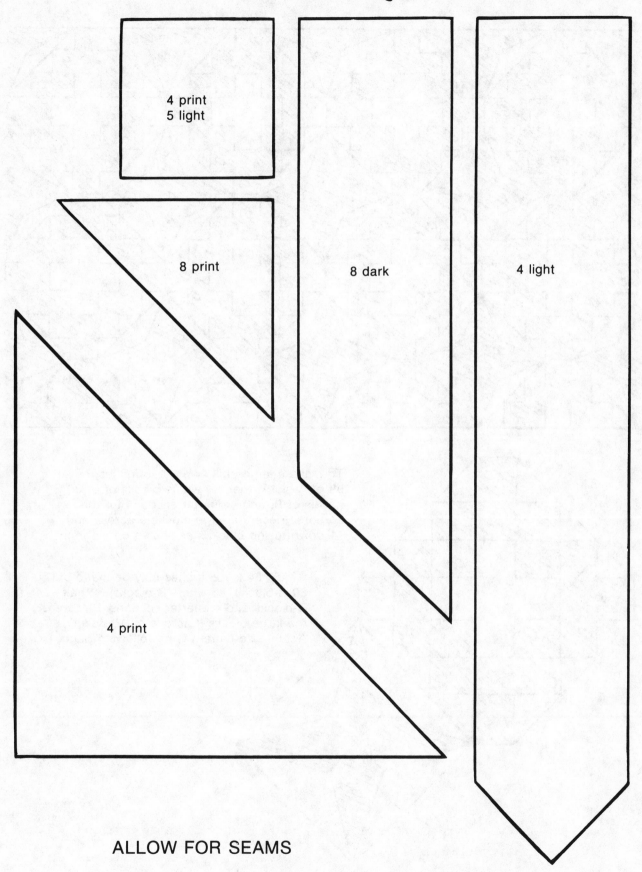

4 print
5 light

8 print

8 dark

4 light

4 print

ALLOW FOR SEAMS

25

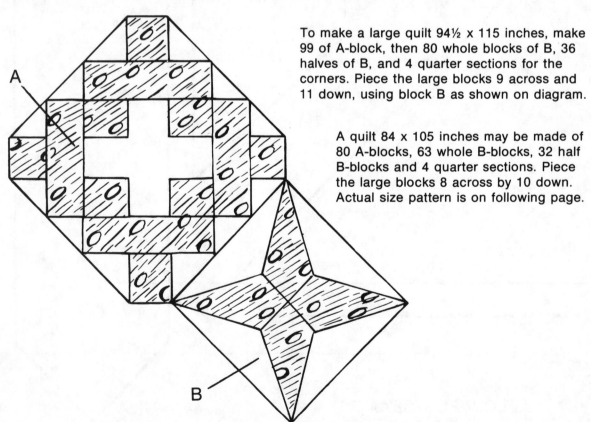

A

B

To make a large quilt 94½ x 115 inches, make 99 of A-block, then 80 whole blocks of B, 36 halves of B, and 4 quarter sections for the corners. Piece the large blocks 9 across and 11 down, using block B as shown on diagram.

A quilt 84 x 105 inches may be made of 80 A-blocks, 63 whole B-blocks, 32 half B-blocks and 4 quarter sections. Piece the large blocks 8 across by 10 down. Actual size pattern is on following page.

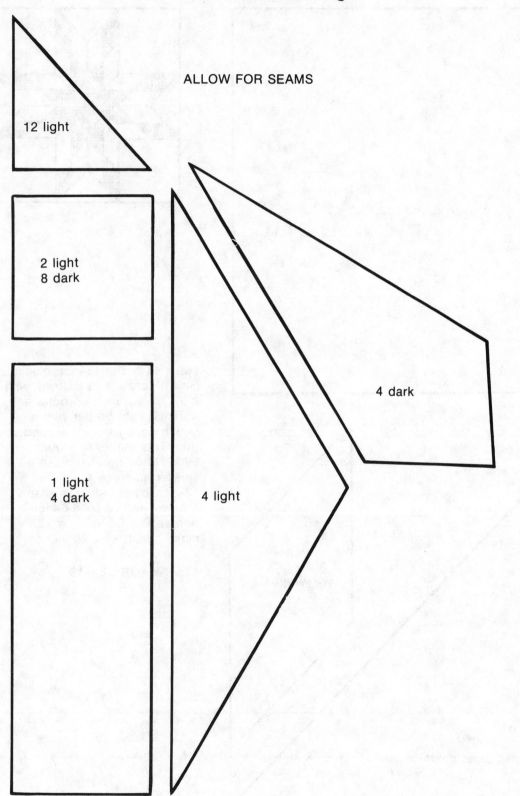

ALLOW FOR SEAMS

12 light

2 light
8 dark

1 light
4 dark

4 light

4 dark

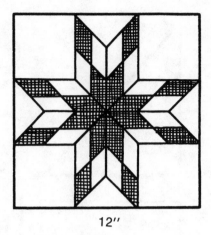

12″

4 background color

8 center
8 tip
16 middle

4 background color

Make 48 of the 12-inch blocks.
Sew 6 across and 8 down, with
a 9-inch border all around or
a 3-inch light border with a
6-inch darker border around
that. This will make a quilt
90 x 114 inches. To make a
smaller quilt use 42 of the
12-inch blocks—6 across and
7 down—with a solid 6-inch
border all around. This will
make a quilt 84 x 96 inches.

ALLOW FOR SEAMS

# The Pinwheel

This is an excellent design for using small prints. Carefully arrange and blend the colors to form the wheel. Use a solid pastel color for the center. White or all one color of very light pastel should be used for the outside pieces of the block. Clip curved seams for smooth fit. Make 48 blocks (6 across, 8 down). These, plus border and 2-inch stripping between blocks, will make a quilt for a double bed.

DO NOT ALLOW FOR SEAMS

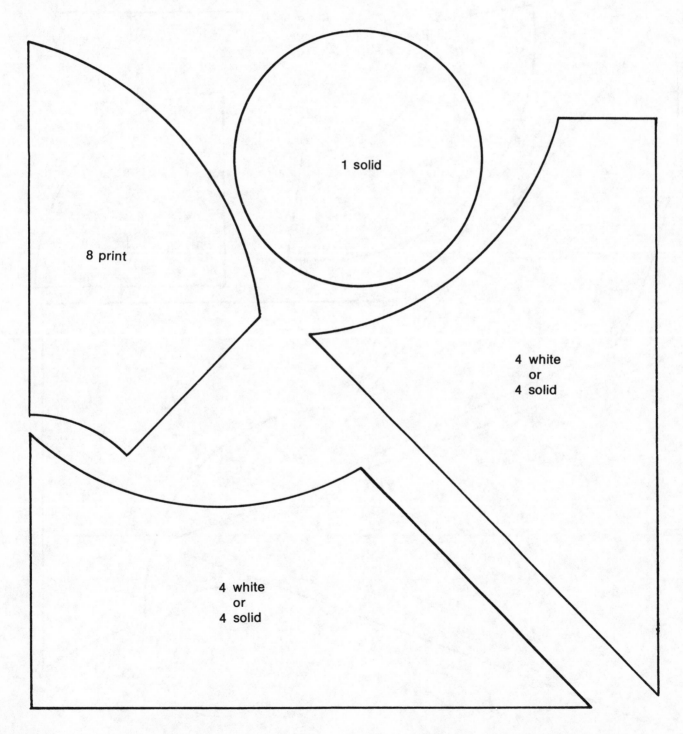

1 solid

8 print

4 white
or
4 solid

4 white
or
4 solid

# Grandmother's Pieced Tulip

Grandmother's Pieced Tulip is a very
dainty design which calls for skill
in piecing. Make 63 blocks for a
full-sized quilt. If you prefer,
you may alternate white blocks with
the pieced ones, in which case you'll
need 32 pieced and 31 white.

DO NOT ALLOW FOR SEAMS

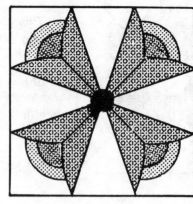

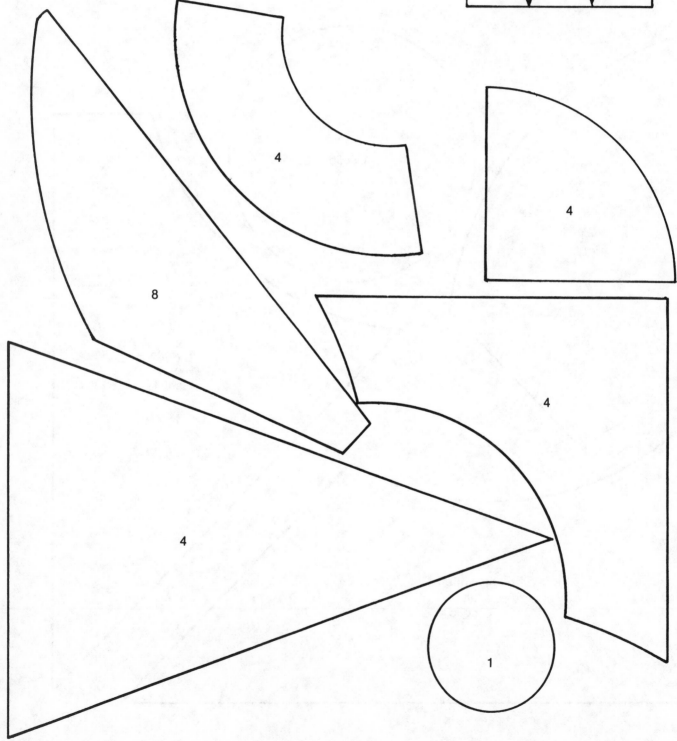

# Double T

Solids make up well for this block. Since it is rather large, you need make only 35 for it looks best when stripped together.

**DO NOT ALLOW FOR SEAMS**

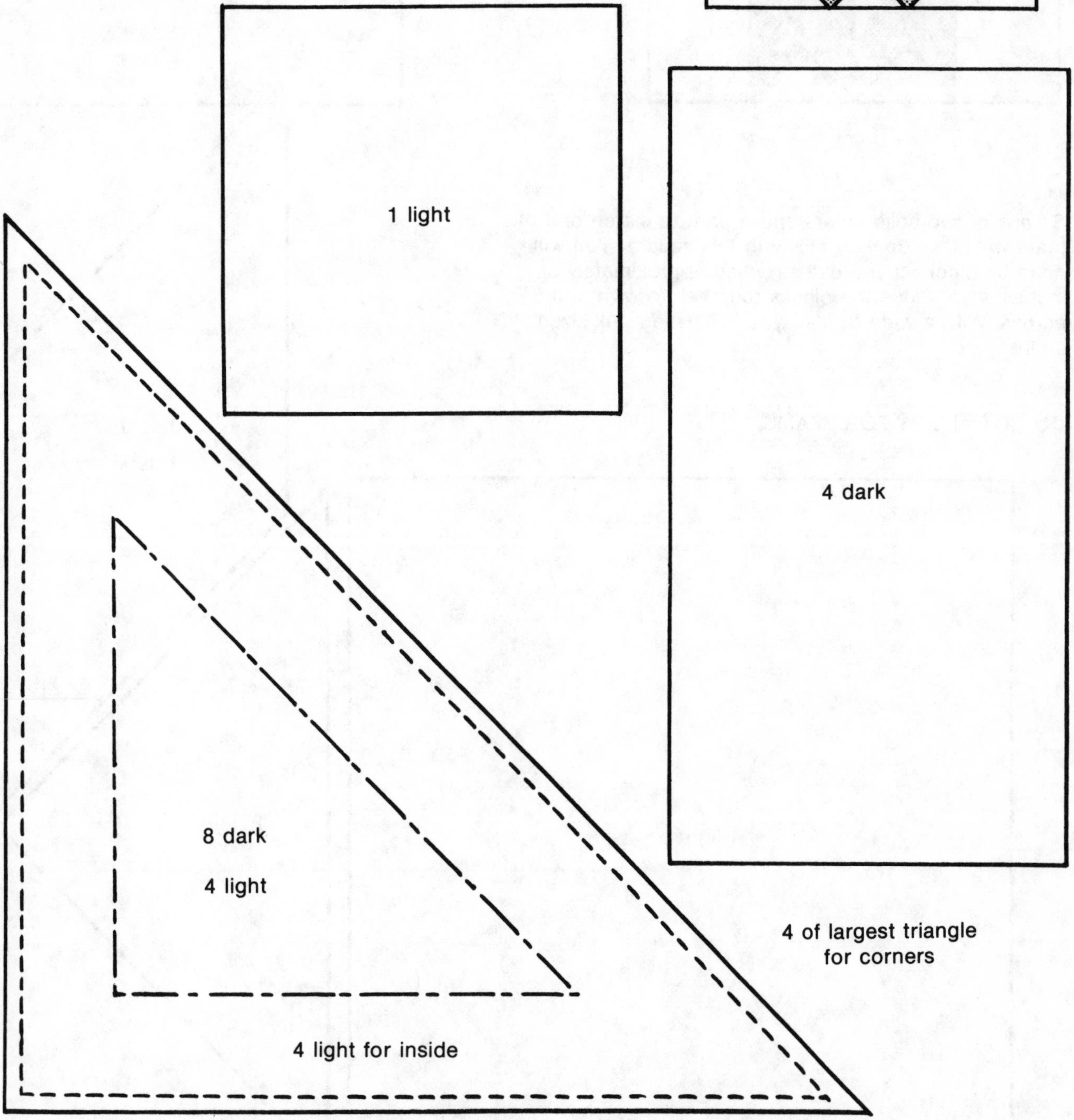

1 light

4 dark

8 dark

4 light

4 light for inside

4 of largest triangle
for corners

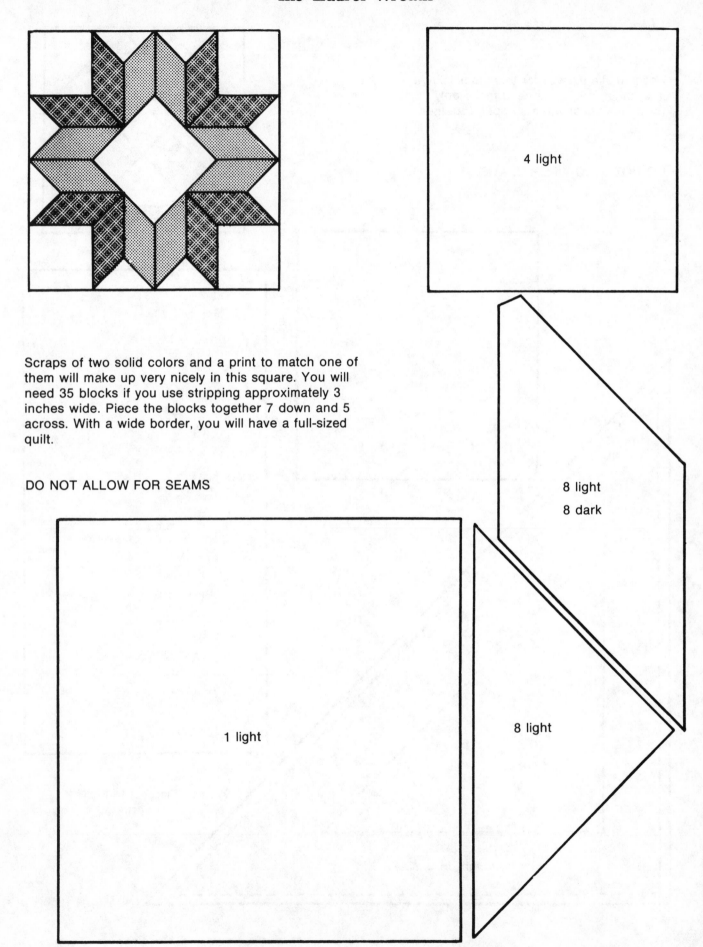

Scraps of two solid colors and a print to match one of them will make up very nicely in this square. You will need 35 blocks if you use stripping approximately 3 inches wide. Piece the blocks together 7 down and 5 across. With a wide border, you will have a full-sized quilt.

DO NOT ALLOW FOR SEAMS

4 light

8 light
8 dark

1 light

8 light

# *Young Man's Fancy*

Dark and light solid colors make up attractively for this block. For a change, make the triangles of print and use solid colors for the squares and rectangles. With stripping, you will need 30 blocks.

DO NOT ALLOW FOR SEAMS

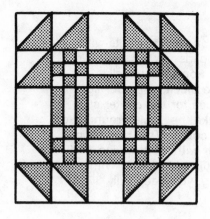

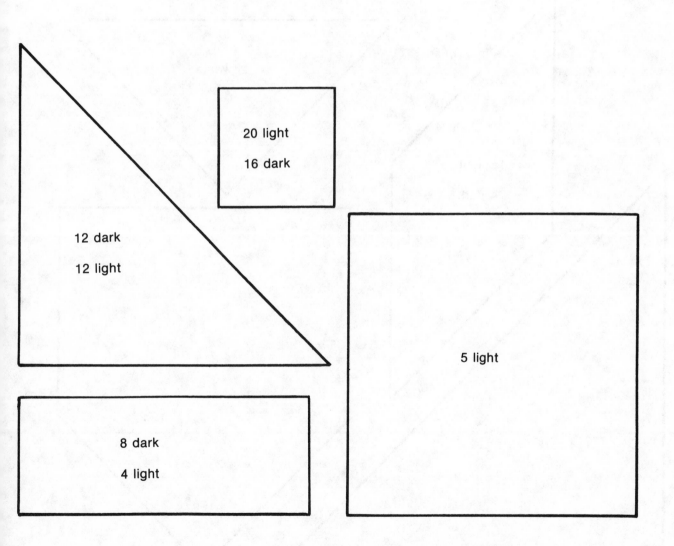

20 light

16 dark

12 dark

12 light

5 light

8 dark

4 light

# Star of Bethlehem

Blend your tiniest prints with pastel solids for this pretty square. For an unusually effective block, use your lightest pieces for the center star and make the circle around it of deeper colors. This may be put together without stripping and will require 42 blocks. With stripping, you need only 30.

DO NOT ALLOW FOR SEAMS

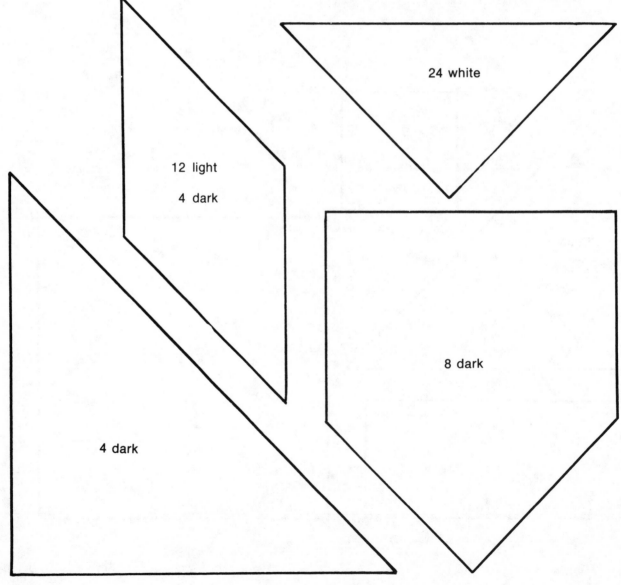

24 white

12 light

4 dark

4 dark

8 dark

# Single Wedding Ring

Only two pattern pieces are needed to make this simple but very effective block. It is a good print-and-solid combination and shows to better advantage when stripped. You may recognize it under one of its other names: Crown of Thorns, Georgetown Circle, or Memory Wreath. Make 48 blocks.

DO NOT ALLOW FOR SEAMS

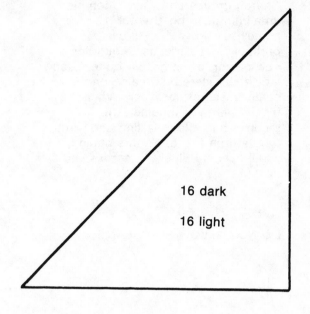

16 dark

16 light

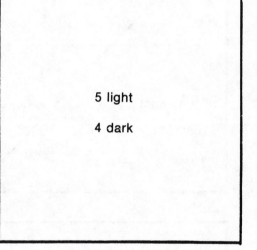

5 light

4 dark

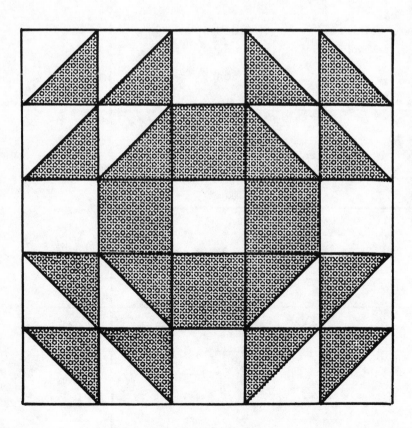

# The Album

Church groups and clubs often piece an album quilt together for a money-raising venture. It was probably first a friendship quilt for a new pastor, or perhaps a bride. Each lady embroidered her name on the center piece of her block. When the blocks were put together, the receiver had a long-lasting and warm tribute from friends. With stripping, you'll need 48 blocks, 6 across and 8 down.

DO NOT ALLOW FOR SEAMS

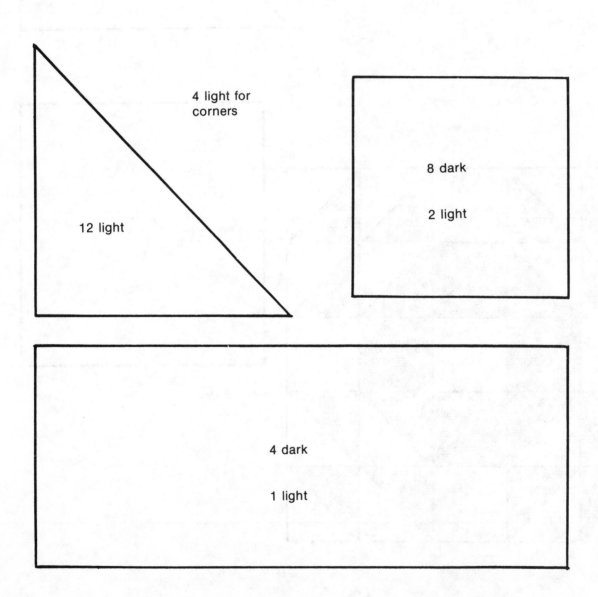

4 light for corners

12 light

8 dark

2 light

4 dark

1 light

# Lily Corners

Dark solids for the base of the tulip with light solids for the top corners combine very attractively with small prints for the tulip points themselves. (The tulips are the eight light diamonds.) Make 63 blocks and strip them together with the same material used to join the four tulips into a square. You will have 9 blocks down and 7 across.

DO NOT ALLOW FOR SEAMS

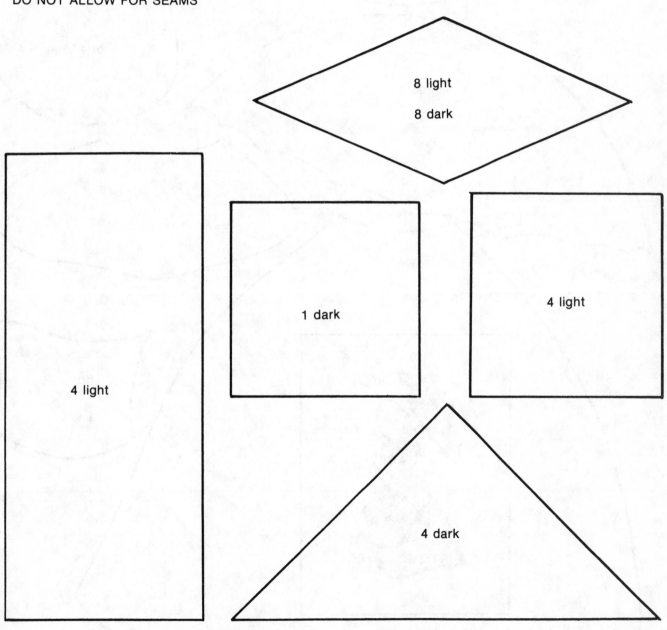

8 light

8 dark

4 light

1 dark

4 light

4 dark

# Sunbonnet Girl

Put Sunbonnet Girl on a 10- x 12-inch white square. Embroider the umbrella handle and arm (pattern given for tracing off arm) and use a chain stitch to make curls. Make 42 blocks and strip them together.

arm to embroider

1 solid

bonnet

1 solid
or 1 print

umbrella

1 print

collar

1 print

skirt

1 print

waist

1 solid

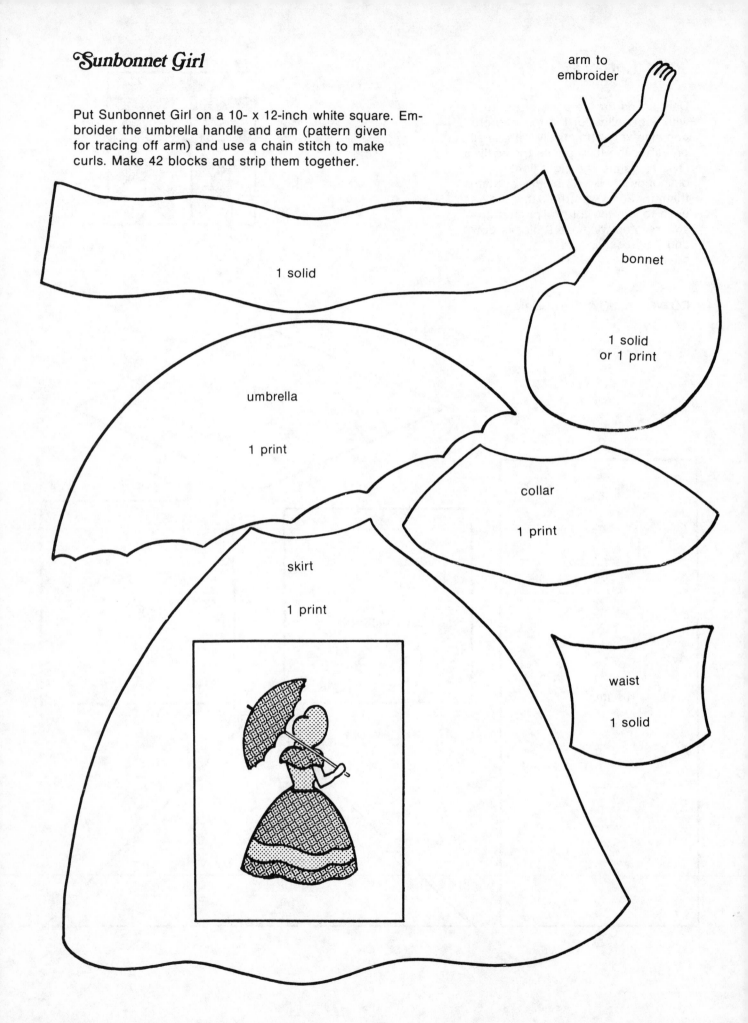

# Straw Hat Boy

Dark and plaid scraps do well for this
busy farmer boy. If possible, use plaid
for his shirt. Cut two narrow pieces and
applique on shirt for straps. Use carbon
paper to trace off the hand and rake and
embroider them in place. These squares
look better when stripped together.
Applique boy on a 20- x 12-inch square of white.
Make 42 squares.

DO NOT ALLOW FOR SEAMS

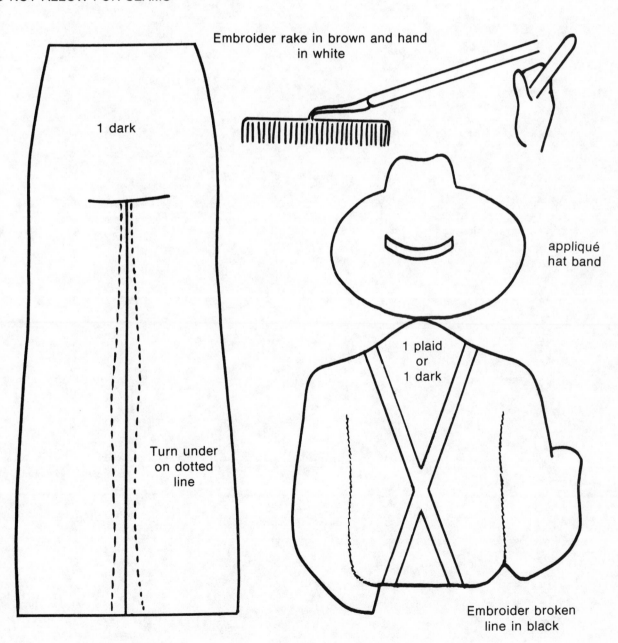

1 dark

Embroider rake in brown and hand
in white

appliqué
hat band

1 plaid
or
1 dark

Turn under
on dotted
line

Embroider broken
line in black